May I Help You?

Kids Talk About Caring

Written by
Pamela Hill Nettleton

Illustrated by
Amy Bailey Muehlenhardt

Thanks to our advisers for their expertise, research, and advice:

Stephanie Goerger Sandahl, M.A., Counseling
Lutheran Social Services of Minnesota, Fergus Falls, Minnesota

Susan Kesselring, M.A., Literacy Educator
Rosemount-Apple Valley-Eagan (Minnesota) School District

PICTURE WINDOW BOOKS
Minneapolis, Minnesota

Managing Editors: Bob Temple, Catherine Neitge
Creative Director: Terri Foley
Editors: Brenda Haugen, Christianne Jones
Editorial Adviser: Andrea Cascardi
Designer: Nathan Gassman
Page production: Picture Window Books
The illustrations in this book were rendered digitally.

Picture Window Books
5115 Excelsior Boulevard
Suite 232
Minneapolis, MN 55416
877-845-8392
www.picturewindowbooks.com

Printed in the United States of America.

Library of Congress Cataloging-in-Publication Data
Nettleton, Pamela Hill.
May I help you? : kids talk about caring / written by Pamela Hill Nettleton ;
    illustrated by Amy Bailey Muehlenhardt.
p. cm. — (Kids talk)
Includes bibliographical references and index.
ISBN 1-4048-0620-2 (reinforced library binding : alk. paper)
1. Caring—Miscellanea—Juvenile literature. I. Muehlenhardt, Amy Bailey, 1974–
    II. Title. III. Series.

BJ1475.N48 2004
177'.7–dc22   2003028242

Dear Kyle,

Whoever had your book last year kept it neat for you, right? What if someone had spilled orange juice in your math book? The pages would be stuck together. Your homework would be all messed up from missing the problems printed on the juicy pages. Yuck!

Your teacher is showing you how to be considerate. It may seem stupid at first, but give it a try! Hey—you could even use really cool paper to cover your book. Then you can make your boring textbook look cool!

Tina

Hello, dear readers! I am Tina Truly, advice columnist to the stars. Well, only if I think of all of you as stars, which I do!

Dear Abby and Ann Landers are my heroines, and I hope to be a professional advice-giver someday. Right now, I'm 13 years old and in seventh grade at Meandering Middle School.

I get all these letters from kids like you asking for help. I write back with my best advice, plus some good ideas from my friends, my big brother Josh, my stepmom, my mom, and my dad. I don't know the answer to every question, but I like trying to figure it out.

In today's column, we're talking about caring. Caring for other people, caring for pets, caring about how well you do in school. You name a topic, and I have a bag full of letters about it! So read on, and see if you agree with my advice.

Sincerely,

Tina Truly

Dear Tina,

My mom and dad are divorced. Some days, my dad seems really mad at my mom. Do I have to be mad at my mom, too? Can I love them both even if they don't like each other?

Shelly

6

Dear Shelly,

I wish I could show you all the letters I get from kids in your situation.

When your mom and dad are mad at each other, it's hard to know how you are supposed to feel. I've been through the same thing. My mom and dad got divorced when I was little.

For a while, it seemed like everyone was mad at my mom. I didn't understand why. It seemed like I wasn't supposed to love my mom anymore. When it was time to go to my mom's house, I felt like I was making my dad mad because I looked forward to seeing her. I missed her, but I was afraid to tell my dad. I thought it would hurt his feelings.

Guess who helped me out? My new stepmom! One day I threw a tantrum. I slammed the door to my room and cried on my bed. My stepmom rubbed my back and told me that she knew this was really hard for me. She told me I didn't have to pick between my mom and dad—I could love them both.

Caring about people you love doesn't stop, even if those people get divorced. I know there are a lot of kids like us out there. You're not alone.

Tina

CLEAN YOUR ROOM!

Dear Tina,

When my mom gets really mad at me, she is so loud.
Does she still love me even while she's yelling at me?

Ryan

8

Dear Ryan,

It's hard to imagine how someone can look so totally grumpy on the outside and still be feeling mushy, nice stuff on the inside, isn't it?

Think of it this way, Ryan. I'll bet you get mad at your mom sometimes, but you still love her, right? When you're done feeling mad, you say you're sorry. Then you feel better. You probably get mad at your best friend, too. By the next day, you usually want to call him up, don't you?

You don't stop loving people when you get mad. We all spend at least a little time being annoyed or angry with people we love. Why? I'm not sure, but it just seems to work that way. So sure, your mom still loves you while she's yelling.

Tina

Dear Tina,

My grandpa always makes me clean my plate because kids somewhere else are hungry. He says I should be happy to have toys because some kids don't have any. He tells me not to complain about my room because other kids are homeless. Am I supposed to take care of everybody?

Tanesha

Dear Tanesha,

It would be nice if you could take care of everybody, but it's just not possible. You should be grateful for everything you have—your loving family, your great room, and all your cool toys. Your grandpa is trying to teach you how to show your gratitude by caring for other people.

Not everyone in the world has enough of what they need, and it's really sad. Since you can't help everyone, maybe you can just help one person at a time. It's not so hard to find something to do to help someone, even if you are a kid.

Maybe you and your grandpa can think up something special to do together. You could collect food and bring it to a food shelf. You could also donate some of your clothes and toys to a homeless shelter. Now go get your grandpa, and tell him some of your awesome ideas!

Tina

Dear Tina,

This is a sad letter. My friend Tony's dad just died. What do I say to Tony when he comes back to school?

Michael

Dear Michael,

We all wonder what to do after someone has died. When my grandpa died, I didn't know what to say to my grandma. We drove up to her house, and I just ran out of the car and gave her a big hug. Grandma just needed to be with people who loved her.

So don't worry, Michael. When Tony comes back to school, he'll know that you and your classmates know what happened. Sit by him at lunch, and see if hanging around together is what he wants right now. Tony might want to talk about losing his dad. He might not.

Tony might feel sad and angry. That's called grieving. Tony will feel better some days and bad on other days. He might even have a tough day a year or two from now. Those are good things for a friend to understand.

Tony will never forget or stop missing his dad. With good friends around him and lots of love from his family, he'll always remember the great things about his dad.

Tina

Dear Tina,

All my sister cares about is playing the piano. She doesn't do anything fun. All she does is practice, practice, practice. How boring! Why doesn't she like stuff I think is cool, like dinosaurs or singing?

Melody

14

Dear Melody,

Sounds like you'd like a sister who is just like you. Maybe another Melody in one family would be fun at first, but after awhile, wouldn't you be *so bored*? Besides, if everyone cared only about what you care about, we'd have a world full of singers who like dinosaurs, and no one would know how to play the piano!

Your sister is probably a fantastic piano player. That sounds cool to me. I'll bet you have learned some great songs from your singing lessons. That makes you sound pretty cool, too. We each get to be cool in our own way because we each care about doing different things.

Here's a neat idea: You and your sister could form your own pop group. You could sing while your sister plays the piano. You could even think of a cool name for your new group. Maybe you could be the "Sassy Sisters." Who knows, you could be the next famous pop group! You'll have to send me an autograph!

Tina

15

Dear Tina,

My mom says I have to take care of my little brother. I have to walk him to school and be sure no big kids pick on him. Why did I get stuck with this job?

Miguel

Dear Miguel,

Let's do an experiment: Pretend your mom didn't ask you to take care of your little brother. You see the school bully giving your little brother a hard time. How do you feel about that? What do you do?

My guess is that you would feel pretty mad at anyone who picked on your brother, even if your mother never asked you to take care of him. I'll bet you want your little brother to be safe on the way to school, too. Your mom asked you to do something you would probably do by yourself anyway.

Why? Because that's how big brothers are. I have one myself. I know I bug Josh a lot. I also know that when I really need him, he'll be there to help me. That's because he cares about me. I know you'll do the same for your brother.

Tina

Dear Tina,

My dad bought me a baseball at a major league game and had a famous baseball player sign it. I have it on a special shelf in my room. I don't want anyone else to touch it. My brother says that's selfish. Is it?

Celia

Dear Celia,

It's great that you take care of your new things. That doesn't mean you're selfish. You care about your new baseball. It's a special gift from your dad, and you want to keep it in a special spot.

Some things are better as display items. When I was younger, my mom bought me a collection of porcelain dolls. I had a princess, a ballerina, a singer, a model, and a doctor. I kept them on their own shelf. I even had individual cases for each one! Even though I'm older now, I still have all the dolls on display in my room. Now the dolls are worth a lot of money, but I would never sell them.

You may not want to share your special baseball with your brother, but you could share some of your other toys with him. I'll bet your brother has something he won't share with you. Find something you and your brother can share or do together.

Tina

Dear Tina,

My sister says that if I had more self-respect, I'd brush my teeth, comb my hair, shower more often, and put my socks in the laundry. What is she talking about?

Anton

Dear Anton,

With all those dirty socks on your bedroom floor, I'm guessing that your bedroom doesn't smell so great. Am I right?

Your sister probably figures you are old enough to care about how you look. Taking showers, combing your hair, and brushing your teeth do a lot of good things for you. They help keep your body healthy. They help you look good to other people. They show that you care about yourself.

Taking care of yourself takes a little time, but it's better than having your sister say you stink. It's also better than getting sick! It's time to clean your act up, Anton.

Tina

Dear Tina,

I have a crush on a boy named Kelly. My mom says it's puppy love, whatever that means. She also says I'm too young to like a boy, but I like him anyway. Am I really too young to like someone?

Maleeka

24

Dear Maleeka,

I had my first crush a few years ago. It wasn't on a boy in my class. It was on Justin Dreamboat, an actor from my favorite TV show, *Space Adventures*. I hung Justin's pictures up all over my bedroom. I used to practice writing his name all over my notebooks. I didn't feel too young to care about him.

Crushes can be fun. Grown-ups sometimes call crushes "puppy love." I think that's their way of saying our crushes aren't the same as the love adults have when they get married. Who wants to get married at our age anyway?

I don't know about you, but I never have very good luck trying to *not* have a feeling. Feelings show up and go away on their own. I can decide what I want to *do* about a feeling, though. Maybe that's what your mom means.

Sometimes kids with crushes tell their friends they are "going together." Your mom might feel you are too young to act like that. Just ask *her*. While you're at it, ask her who her first crush was!

Tina

Dear Tina,

I love my cat Pablo so much, but my sister has allergies. We have to get rid of Pablo. Can we get rid of my sister instead?

Armand

Dear Armand,

Tempting idea, isn't it? Sorry, Armand, but your sister is here to stay. Caring about a pet is important, but caring about your sister comes first.

It is really tough to give up something you care about so much. I'll bet your sister feels bad about giving Pablo away, too. Since pets have a way of belonging to the whole family, I'll bet even your parents are sad. But trust me—allergies are crummy.

Telling your family how bad you feel about losing Pablo may help you through this. Maybe you can have a family meeting about what to do. You might be able to visit Pablo at his new home. You might even be able to get a pet your sister isn't allergic to, like a fish or turtle.

I've found families can be pretty smart about thinking up ways to solve problems. Ask yours for a little help.

Tina

**Here's a quiz about caring. Grab a pencil and some paper.
Don't worry! It's just for fun.**

1. Stepmoms:
   A. sometimes have some good advice.
   B. always have warts on their noses.
   C. are really mean.

2. When you feel mad at a friend you:
   A. go buy him a gift.
   B. eat liver for breakfast.
   C. eventually get over it.

3. If you want to make the world a better place:
   A. give up. It can't happen.
   B. try to do it all at once.
   C. start small, but think big.

4. What you love to do:
   A. is what makes you special.
   B. has to be approved by your sister.
   C. should be the same as what everyone else loves to do.

5. Big brothers are good for:
   A. nothing.
   B. helping out little brothers and sisters.
   C. taking the blame whenever you do something wrong.

6. If your brother wants to play with your special baseball, you should:
   A. throw it at him.
   B. ignore him.
   C. share something else with him instead.

7. When your bedroom smells like a hamster, you should:
   A. spray perfume on your slippers.
   B. take a shower now and then.
   C. get more hamsters.

8. Puppy love means:
   A. two dogs get married.
   B. two cats get married.
   C. having a crush on someone.

9. If you have a crush on a famous TV star, he'll:
   A. come over to play video games.
   B. wave at you from the TV.
   C. be someone your brother teases you about for a while.

10. People can be allergic to:
    A. little sisters.
    B. pets.
    C. math tests.

Answer Key: 1-A, 2-C, 3-C, 4-A, 5-B, 6-C, 7-B, 8-C, 9-C, 10-B

Being a nurse seems like a cool job, and it's all about caring. Florence Nightingale helped nurses gain respect. She was born in Italy and grew up in England. She was a wealthy and educated young woman. Florence did not have to work, but she wanted to help people. She visited homes of sick people and became interested in nursing. She attended a nursing school in Germany.

In 1854, Britain, France, and Turkey fought in a war with Russia. Hospitals for the soldiers were dirty, smelly, and full of germs. Florence brought 38 nurses to Turkey to help. She found sick soldiers wearing bloody uniforms. They had no blankets and slept in yucky tents. There were no supplies for cleaning or treating the sick.

Florence had ideas about how to make all of this better, but the male doctors wouldn't listen to her. They gave her a hard time, but she won them over when they saw how much she cared about the sick soldiers. Florence raised money to help get supplies to the hospitals. She kept the hospitals clean, and soldiers started to get better.

When Florence went home to England, she was a hero. She continued to work. She wrote books teaching women how to be better nurses. She showed the country how to make hospitals healthier. Florence helped start the first nursing school in England. She died in 1910.

Florence could have led an easy life, but instead she took action to improve the health of soldiers and people around the world. All it took was a little caring.

Words to Know

Here are some of my favorite words and expressions from today's letters.

advice—suggestions from people who think they know what you should do about a problem

allergies—having a reaction like a runny nose, teary eyes, or maybe even a rash when you're around certain things; people can have allergies to things like plants, animals, or dust

divorce—when married people split up

expert—a person who knows a ton of stuff about something

grieving—feeling really sad or angry after someone you love dies

stepmom—the woman who marries your dad if something happens to your mom

To Learn More

At the Library

Bender, Marie. *Caring Counts.* Edina, Minn.: ABDO, 2002.

Doak, Robin. *Caring.* Austin, Texas: Raintree Steck-Vaughn, 2002.

Rice, David L. *Because Brian Hugged His Mother.* Nevada City, Calif.: Dawn Publications, 1999.

On the Web

FactHound offers a safe, fun way to find Web sites related to this book. All of the sites on FactHound have been researched by our staff. *www.facthound.com*

1. Visit the FactHound home page

2. Enter a search word related to this book, or type in this special code: 1404806202.

3. Click on the FETCH IT button.

Your trusty FactHound will fetch the best Web sites for you!

Index

Books in This Series

- **Do I Have To? Kids Talk About Responsibility**
- **How Could You? Kids Talk About Trust**
- **I Can Do It! Kids Talk About Courage**
- **Is That True? Kids Talk About Honesty**
- **Let's Get Along! Kids Talk About Tolerance**
- **May I Help You? Kids Talk About Caring**
- **No Fair! Kids Talk About Fairness**
- **Pitch In! Kids Talk About Cooperation**
- **Treat Me Right! Kids Talk About Respect**
- **Want to Play? Kids Talk About Friendliness**
- **We Live Here Too! Kids Talk About Good Citizenship**
- **You First! Kids Talk About Consideration**